Tom Maxwell and Dr. Charles Olawuyi

Golden path

To success

The greatest discovery in life. The success myths, your perspective to money, the ultimate principle and your understanding about time.

By

**Tom Maxwell.
Dr. Charles Olawuyi.**

GOLDEN PATH TO SUCCESS

copyright@2022
All Right Reserved

Tom Maxwell and Dr. Charles Olawuyi

TABLE OF CONTENTS

CHAPTER ONE 1
    THE BEGINNING 1
CHAPTER TWO 5
    THE MIND OF A SUCCESSFUL MAN 5
        Knowing How to Become Successful 5
        The Success Myth 6
        YOUR PERSPECTIVE MATTERS 9
CHAPTER THREE 11
    HOW TO BE A SUCCESSFUL INVESTOR 11
CHAPTER FOUR 17
    THE ULTIMATE PRINCIPLE 17
CHAPTER FIVE 23
    How To Get Coach. 23
CHAPTER SIX 27
    LET TIME WORK FOR YOUR MONEY 27
CHAPTER SEVEN 31
    LET TIME WORK FOR YOUR MONEY II 31

CHAPTER ONE

THE BEGINNING

Have confidence that if you have done a little thing well you can do a bigger thing well.

The greatest discovery you can ever make in your life is that of uncovering who you really are and what you have been purposed by God to accomplish while you are on the planet earth.

The fear of the Lord is the beginning of knowledge (Proverb 1:7) and authority without wisdom is like a heavy axe without an edge, fitter to bruise than polished. The empires of the future are empires of the mind. So when your mind determines your destination, your heart will design the map on how to reach it.

Once you are able to search your mind out apply yourself to your calling. God will begin to unfold layers of talents that you never imagined you possess. Therefore, discover your purpose and unearth your gift.

GOLDEN PATH TO SUCCESS

Your gifts are to be employed to fulfill your purpose on earth. Remember; "Your state of mind create your state of result".

Get informed that your level of knowledge determines your level of fulfillment. And your increase in life is determined by the amount of things that flow out of you. God is a God of potential. " **Big Thinking Precedes Great Achievement".** God is not interested in what you have accomplished; but he is interested in what is left inside of you that He desperately wants you to manifest. So the capacity of your potential is not determine by what you have or what others think about.

Get focused and never give up. Always remember that life is not fair - get used to it that circumstances and crisis are God's tool to move you into your purpose and maximizing of your potential. Believe it can be done. When you believe something can be done. Your mind will find the ways to do it. Believing a solution paves the way to solution. Eliminate "impossibility, won't, can't do" from your thinking and speaking vocabularies. Don't let traditions paralyses your mind; Ask yourself this daily. How can I do better? There is no limit to self-improvement. When you ask yourself, sound answer will appear. Try it and see!

I have six honest serving men. They taught me all I know their names were: "Where, What, When, Why, How and Who". This is the attitude and principle on which I leave. Attitude is a choice. Attitude tune - up important to maintaining a healthy and winning formula through serving God and His kingdom. Serving God is a door to glorious tomorrow.

CHAPTER TWO

THE MIND OF A SUCCESSFUL MAN

Knowing How to Become Successful.

The power and knowledge of how to become successful is more valuable than success itself. The knowledge of how to become rich is more important than riches. This implies that those who desire success in their life must endeavor to seek out the formula which must be apply in order to achieve their ambition of changing their fortune.

The key is that: once you know how to become successful, you're already successful; meaning that you could easily implement the success plan a million times over and still achieve the same result without losing your way in the maze.

The challenge of becoming successful is to seek and locate the route to success, not the success itself.

The Success Myth.
Many people have wrong notion on the functions of success, reasons for which people become rich. Some of the identified factors which do not contribute to success in life include;

GOLDEN PATH TO SUCCESS

Age

You don't become successful because you are old or elderly. Age is neither a guarantee nor factor in becoming Successful. Evidence abounds of young rich men and poor old men and vice versa. You can be successful at any particular age through the application of time trusted principle and not age.

Gender

A number of women lament their inability to make it in life saying: 'It is a man's world'. Fortunately, gender has absolutely nothing to contribute in your being successful. Men and women across the globe are rich and poor. Success is not gender friendly. In Order words, Success is gender blind. Those who are successful do what leads to success and the women who apply the same principles equally post success for their efforts.

Race

The color of your skin, tribe, where you hail from is not a function of success in any endeavor. Being White or Black is not a contributory factor to what you could eventually become.

Location

The fact that you are in America, Asia, Europe or Africa is not what will determine whether you'll achieve success or not. There are successful people all across the world regardless of countries or continent.

The Realities

The realities of being successful is that no matter who you are, where you come from, where you live and the color of your skin. You could become successful by

GOLDEN PATH TO SUCCESS

analyzing the right principles. The success principles involve around the individual: Who he is, what he does, how he does it and etc.

The principles are many but these are the key ones that bear more on the personality of success than other factors.

Don't Accept No for An Answer.

You must strive to prevail and surmount the odds in your environment in order to reach your destination which is success. As such, it is the internal factors with you that will guarantee you success not your location, gender or age. Eliminate **no I can't** in your thinking and speech, instead use words like **I can, I will** and you shall succeed.

Fill a Need

The creation of value will make you to succeed.

Create value and become rich. There is no system, be it political, economic, social or military that can resist someone who can produce value. Many have become rich by creating value that solved one problem or the other for the society. When you create solution for your environment, it becomes an avenue for you to become successful.

YOUR PERSPECTIVE MATTERS.
To succeed, you must have the perspective of a successful person. The perspective of a successful person is not what he could derive from a particular situation but what he could do to make the situation better. If you think constantly in that direction, success will be yours. So change your perspective!

Practice asking and listening. Get stimulated! Associate with people who can help you think of new ideas, new ways of doing things. You will succeed!

CHAPTER THREE

HOW TO BE A SUCCESSFUL INVESTOR

Every investor should have '**The Investor's Anthology**'. It's a compilation of original ideas from the investment industry's greatest minds, featuring familiar name like Buffett, Fisher, Keynes and Graham.

> "Not all investors have the innate or acquired personal characteristics that are mandatory to succeed in building a portfolio that will significantly outperform the market over the years".

What are the tracts required for success as aggressive investors? (The strategic investor published in 1963) Five points were outlines.

PATIENCE

The aggressive Investor should not expect quick results although occasionally this occurs. Success depends on large measure on the ability to select undervalued situations not currently recognized by the majority of investors and to wait for expected developments...... that may only come after several years.

How true? Short term, a share price will move for a whole host of reasons. Long term through the share price direction will correlate to the company's profitability.

COURAGE

The investor must have solid conviction and the

GOLDEN PATH TO SUCCESS

courage an confidence emanating from them that is courage at times to ignores those who disagree.

There is no shortage of opinion within the market. However, determining whose judgment you should listen to on a regular basis is a futile task. Instead, it's far better to spend time using your own experience to form your own conclusion.

Undervalued shares almost always have a cloud of gloom hanging over them, with many experts on hand to supply a negative opinion. However, investing in visible day to day businesses, whose products or services are not subjected to rapid change or decline, will help provide the necessary courage whenever a falling share price is telling you something.

INTELLIGENCE

To realize success, the aggressive investor must possess average level of intelligence, but by no means does he need to be a genius.

A common sense big picture view will help you from wandering aimlessly in maze of details.

Surely, something as difficult as beating the stock market requires a brain - taxing, sophisticated approach. The best investment tends to come from obviously good businesses bought on obviously cheap valuation.

EMOTIONAL STABILITY

This trait is needed to prevent the investor from being engulfed in waves of optimism and pessimism that periodically sweep over wall street.

A key task for any successful investor is to separate fact from emotion. Good old human nature creating bouts of excessive greed and fear can become a real danger to your portfolio.

Emotional stability will prevent over excitement

GOLDEN PATH TO SUCCESS

from market rises and depression from market falls.

HARD WORK

To be successful, an aggressive investor must do thorough research which requires considerable time and effort.

There are no short cuts to stock market glory. Even such simple tenets as 'lock for obviously good businesses' require investigation and research.

CHAPTER FOUR

THE ULTIMATE PRINCIPLE

GOLDEN PATH TO SUCCESS

...... Will a man rob God? Yet you rob me. But you ask. How can we rob you? "In tithe and offering"

You are under a curse - the whole nation of you because you are robbing me. Bring the whole tithe into the storehouse, that there may be food in my house.

"Test me in this, says the Lord Almighty and see if I will not throw open the floodgates of heaven and pour out so much blessing that you will not have room enough for it.

This is why a lot of people experience losses in their business or project. It is because you've violated the most fundamental principle of supernatural prosperity from God to a better life.

This principle works on the law of causes and effects. If you apply a principle correctly, you will get the expected result, it doesn't matter about your status and if the principle is broken, you will get the results as well. Therefore, success and failure is predictable.

The Mathematician principle of calculation is $1 \times 1 = 1$, $1 + 1 = 2$ and $1 - 1 = 0$. It is universal, that is how it has been and how it will forever be till the world comes to an end. The principle is unquestionable but acceptable.

If you want to develop your muscles, you have to do what your instructor asks you to do and in a short while you would have built the layer muscle you desire. Therefore, everything is build or established on one principle.

God build the world on principles and that is why you don't have to pray for the sun to rise and set. For the stars to appear, for the oxygen to flow into your system, for day to break and night to fall. He is not a God of confusion. He is not moody God who blesses people as he pleases. Once you follow the principles he

GOLDEN PATH TO SUCCESS

has laid down in any area of your life, you will surely get the desired results. But the problem is that most of us crave for miracles: What you need is principles on how to sustain the miracle and God will entrust His riches in your hands abundantly.

God is the source of all money and that money is a spirit with wings. He will not entrust you with his wealth if you have not mastered the principle governing wealth creation. God will not entrust His wealth to people who can't avoid waste.

Avoid waste and be trustworthy so that God will entrust his riches in your hands.

God says: Give me only ten percent of the total money that flows into your pocket and those blessings, miracle of prosperity will be yours.

- One, God says He will bless you beyond what you can measure.
- Two, He will not allow you to suffer losses.

- Three, He will not allow you to face financial crises.

- Four, He will allow divine blessings to flow into your direction at due seasons.

- Fifth, He will cause your game and wealth to spread beyond the shore of your country.

All these are for you if you can abide by that ultimate principle. And if you chose to break the principle, what you will get is the REVERSE of the benefits. Always abide by the principles and you will succeed. Remember, God is not a law breaker; He cannot break His own principles.

GOLDEN PATH TO SUCCESS

CHAPTER FIVE

How To Get Coach.

Successful people are usually very busy individual. Everybody wants to meet with them, shake hands with them, wine and dine with them. They may not be able to meet everyone who would like to associate with them. But they are ready to share their secret with those who are worthy of their attention. Note, not all will be willing but 70% of them are willing. So the question is : how do you work your way to becoming worthy of

GOLDEN PATH TO SUCCESS

their attention?

The ultimate rule is "Give and you shall receive". It is very unfortunate that many want to receive without Giving. It is a spiritual principle which cannot be broken.

The lesson is this: You should try to give before you expect to receive. My experience with a mentor of mine when I wanted to link up myself to him. It was very tough and rough but I never give up. I have written several series of letters to him and none was acknowledged. But an idea came to my mind one afternoon after, I have just read my holy book (Bible) that: there is blessing in Giving than receiving. I prayed about this and the following day I went to a shop I bought two books and other items and dispatched them to him through the courier to his office.

A month later, I bought two expensive shirts, ties and two pairs of trousers to match and I dispatched them to his office through the same means.

Weeks later, I wrote a letter requesting to have an appointment with him. Believe me the man left a standing instruction that once I surfaced, they should bring me to his office and since that very day we've been best of friends. Therefore, you have to give if you must received

Don't be a parasite protégé. Try to know what your mentor's needs are and Go out to meet whichever you can. Make friends with their secretary and personal assistants.

Another ethical suggestion is that: Be sensitive to your mentor's time. Successful people value their time and won't appreciate anyone who appears not to respect their time. Before you meet your mentor for anything, get your questions ready. Listen to him and don't interrupt his message because he probably knows whatever you may want to ask.

Remember, working with a good coach in your area of interest can increase your area of interest and

GOLDEN PATH TO SUCCESS

increase your speed to the top and save you from costly and embarrassing mistakes.

CHAPTER SIX
LET TIME WORK FOR YOUR MONEY.

There was this great saying: That **"Time is Money"**. Yes, time is money only for those who see possibilities before they become obvious and the future belong to them.

Let me also say that God does not want us to do extraordinary things. He only required us to do ordinary things extraordinarily well.

Those people you considered wealthy today did not get to that position overnight; they started by taking one step. They know that over time that single step will produce giant result. If one advance confidently in the direction of his dreams, and endeavors to live the life which he has imagined. He will surely meet with success unexpectedly in common hours.

It is a pity that: A lot of people have missed out in life by refusing to take that single step. Many want to start their business only when they have a lot of money. Believe this: Time is the only resource you need to become a millionaire. You don't have to be born with silver spoon. You don't have to come from a wealthy background. You don't need any special advantage to enable you to climb the millionaire ladder. Time is all you need and interestingly time is all you have.

The rich and the poor both have same numbers of hours available to them in a day. The difference between rich people and poor people is the way they use their time and in what direction they are headed every single day.

Time is the universal currency of the world. It is not the American dollar; It is not the British Pound Sterling. Once you master the use of your time, you have control over your destiny.

Embrace shaving and avoid spending and if you must spend. Spend your money wisely. A lot of people make budget on bills payment without any preference for the percentage that would be saved for their future purpose after their retirement.

Always plan your expenditure; those wealthy people you see today plan their expenditure with time value. Did you know that one dollar put away in savings constantly over time can produce amazing result. Did you know that $20, $50 and $100 you waste on a daily bases, of they are been save can generate $7300, $18250, $36500 respectively in one calendar year and $36500, $91250, $182500 respectively in five years without the bank interest. And I believe you can do more than that. Now imagine how rich you will become within that period.

GOLDEN PATH TO SUCCESS

Take the step today, don't be afraid, and don't delay. Start the process today with what you have, let your time work for your money. Remember success is a journey of discovery and adventure.

CHAPTER SEVEN

LET TIME WORK FOR YOUR MONEY II

Every stage in life has its own peculiar needs and requirements but hardly is there any individual who does not need a prosperous retirement. But unfortunately, most people after having a good life within early and middle years suddenly found themselves not with Gold in their old age.

But expert says this won't be if every individual embrace a life - centered financial investment planning. And it can be done if one develops personal interest in investment matters.

The basic strategy of financial planning involves setting financial goals after taking out time to understand and consider the peculiar financial needs, one is likely to encounter at each stage of one's life. It also involves identifying the peculiar investment instruments that would fit into one's financial pattern at

GOLDEN PATH TO SUCCESS

every stage.

Basically, a typical working adult life possess through three different phases.

(1) He is first unmarried, aged between 17 - 35 years.

(2) Later he has a growing family, between 35 - 44 years.

(3) And by the time he clock 60.

This time the children are gone to start their own life cycle; he is left alone with his spouse or alone. Warren Buffett, don of investment says that young unmarried age is the best time to invest in equities of public companies, trading in the equities market is high paying. We need to take risks, sometimes we succeed. Sometime we fail. Failure encourages us to make more risk and the cycle continues until we succeed. Young investors can afford to have their equities investment on long-term.

By the middle years, an investor may find it unnecessary to start diverting funds into real estate, at least to secure a comfortable home for the family if not for anything else. The best within the middle years according to Paul Allen and W. Buffett is investing in treasury bills. Treasury bill is a short time security usually 90 days, this provide regular and secure income that would aid a retired person with few other income sources in meeting regular financial obligations even while the original capital is preserved.

Therefore, everything you see as really great and inspiring is created by the individual who can labor in freedom. So the earlier you set out, the earlier you are likely to get to your goal and that with maximum ease and minimum discomfort; it is like taking a long distance walk to a predetermined destination according to Vivian Horler of personal financial of South Africa.

GOLDEN PATH TO SUCCESS

One of the greatest mistakes we make in life is not to have started planning early enough. Most young people especially students hardly invest while in school. Instead, they fritter away any "excess" money that comes their ways on fads and trivialities just to be in stop with the Joneses. So by the time they get into early or middle adult life.

Consider this, assuming interest rate remain unchanged at 12 per cent, a man who wants to have $1 million by the age of 65 would ONLY have to put aside $23 a month from the age of 20 to achieve that goal. However, if he leaves it until when he is 40, the cost would have risen up to $266 a month and by the time he wake up at 60, he would need nothing less than $6 125 a month to achieve that goal.

Why wasting of time? Why not start now? A determined soul will do more with a rusty wrench than others will accomplish with all the tools of a machine shop. No one is less ready for tomorrow than the person who holds the most rigid belief about what tomorrow will contain according to Watts Wacker.

www.ingramcontent.com/pod-product-compliance
Lightning Source LLC
Chambersburg PA
CBHW050323220526
45465CB00005B/2100